DATE DUE

# CONVERSATIONS ON CONTEMPORARY DRAMA

# CONVERSATIONS ON CONTEMPORARY DRAMA

BY

## CLAYTON HAMILTON

MEMBER OF THE NATIONAL INSTITUTE OF ARTS AND LETTERS

*34288*

*A Series of Nine Lectures,*
*Delivered in Earl Hall, at Columbia University,*
*from February 11 to April 7, 1924.*

New York
THE MACMILLAN COMPANY
1924

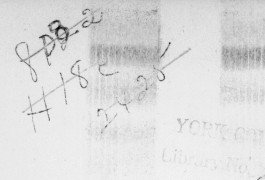

TO

THE THOUSANDS OF STUDENTS,

AT COLUMBIA AND ELSEWHERE,

WHO, FOR TWENTY YEARS, HAVE LISTENED

TO MY TALKS ABOUT THE DRAMA.

# PREFACE

HERE is a book that was not written at a desk, but improvised upon a lecture-platform in the presence of an audience. It is a stenographic record of a series of informal lectures delivered in Earl Hall, at Columbia University, on nine successive Monday mornings, from February 11 to April 7, 1924.

When it was announced that this course would be open to the public, my friend Mr. George P. Brett, the President of The Macmillan Company, told me that he would like to publish the lectures in a volume. Mr. Brett had never heard me talk in public; and I perceived that he had assumed that I was a lecturer, of the sort that we so frequently import from London, who, appearing on the platform with a printed or typewritten pamphlet, proceeds to read it from the outset to the end, and, having done so, travels elsewhere, to read the same text to another audience. I hastened to explain that my public talks were not lectures in the formal sense, but merely conversations, that I carried nothing to the platform except the ideas in my head and the watch in my hand, that I improvised my conversations as I went along, and that whether I happened to be good or not depended mainly on the reaction of the audience. Since I did not plan my lectures in advance and rarely remembered an hour afterward anything that I had said, I could see no way to furnish Mr. Brett with the volume he was kind enough to wish to publish.

But Mr. Brett is a persistent gentleman, who is not accustomed to be thwarted in his purposes. He immediately offered to send a stenographer up to Earl Hall to take down every word that I said, and he suggested that, with a little editing, these stenographic reports could be prepared for publication. It was Mr. Brett's idea that, in this period of university extension, many people who might have liked to attend such a course of lectures if they had lived within commuting distance of Columbia University might like to have a record of the lectures made available to them in print.

I received this suggestion with considerable perturbation, because it seemed to controvert the only conscience that ever really troubles me,—the conscience of the craftsman. For twenty years I had practiced the two professions of lecturing and writing; but, in all that time, I had never written a single paragraph that I intended to speak nor dictated a single paragraph that I intended to print. I explained to Mr. Brett that writing was one thing and talking was another, that the technical processes of the two professions were entirely distinct, that my best writing would be unspeakable and my best talking would be unreadable; but he countered this argument with the suggestion that, if all my other books contained a record of my writing, there was no particular reason why this one book should not contain a record of my speaking.

After considerable hesitance, I agreed to try the plan as an experiment. I was afraid that I might suffer from stage-fright if I ever paused to realize that everything that I was saying was being taken down in shorthand and might subsequently be used against me; and it was, therefore, arranged that the stenographer should hide herself in the audience so that I should not see her and might forget that she was there. During the first lecture, I was a little worried and, every now and then, became too fussy with my phraseology for fear of the stenographer; but, after that, I actually managed to forget that the recording angel was present with poised pencil and to swing into my natural habit of talking to the audience without self-consciousness.

To read the stenographic records seemed as strange to me at first as the experience of hearing my own voice upon the phonograph or seeing my own figure on the motion picture screen. I had never known before exactly how I talked. I had always known that my manner of speaking was very different from my style of writing; for, in following the two professions, I had deliberately practiced different methods for the attainment of different ends. But I had never had an opportunity before to analyze exactly the various distinctions between the two technical methods of expression.

In writing for the printed page, the craftsman strives for literary finish, for finality of form; but this effect must be carefully avoided in talking to an audience. I have found in practice that the only expedient by which I can hold the attention of an audience for an hour is an appearance of unfettered spontaneity. This is the reason why I never plan a lecture in advance. I want, of course, to know enough about the subject to be able to talk about it at least five times as long as the lecture is to last; I want to know the leading points that I am likely to discuss, and the probable order in which I shall take them up; but I do not want to know beforehand the arrangement of details, and I try always to catch the mood which is to dominate the conversation from experimenting with the audience. My only notebook is the dial of my watch: as the minute hand goes round, I proportion my points accordingly.

The expression of the same idea is more compact in writing than in speaking. A thought which, on the printed page, would receive complete expression in one hundred words may require three or four hundred words for presentation on the lecture-platform. Because of the physical effort involved in listening, an audience cannot take in an idea that is expressed too briefly. For this reason, talk is necessarily thinner in its thought-content than writing. Repetition, which the writer especially avoids, must be practiced by the speaker as a technical expedient. He can see by looking at his auditors whether or not they have completely grasped the point he is expounding; and, if they have not grasped it, he must subtly manage to repeat himself without letting them perceive that he is doing so. Such a subterfuge is not necessary on the printed page. The writer may compact his thought into a single carefully written sentence; for this single sentence will stand there on the page, to be looked at whenever the reader may find it necessary to refer to it again.

The audience is an active collaborator in any lively lecture. A point that goes well with the audience will suggest others that are similar and will often tempt the speaker to digress from the main path of his discourse; and, on the other hand, an indication from the audience that the talk is growing dull may often require a sudden change of mood and an alteration of the plan of the attack. It is these acrobatics which are unforeseen that give a zest to lecturing and differentiate it from the more methodical and steadfast task of literary composition.

The writer, if his work is going badly, can lay his pen aside at any moment and try again another day; but the lecturer must keep on talking until his hour is up. Even when his thoughts come haltingly, he must never hesitate in his discourse; for, if he begins to fumble around for words, the auditors will be afflicted with that feeling of distress which arises from a subconscious desire to help him out. The speaker, therefore, must employ the readiest method of expression, even when he knows that it is not the best; he has no time to edit or rewrite a sentence in his mind while he is progressing from the initial capital to the terminal period. For this reason, the rhythm of speech is more brisk, more staccato, more headlong in its onward rush than the more deliberately modulated rhythm of written prose.

In preparing these stenographic records for the press, I have deleted a few digressions and cut out a few repetitions; but, in the main, I have left the text unaltered. I have made no attempt to rewrite it in literary terms. My other books were deliberately written to be read; but this book is frankly an experiment in the broadcasting of unpremeditated speech from the lecture-platform to a distant audience.

The name of the stenographer who took these lectures down is Miss Katherine King. I regret to say that I have never met her personally and should not recognize her if she should be sitting in the seat beside me the next time that I attend the theatre. But, whatever Mr. Brett may think of the result of our collaboration, it gives me a curious sensation to reflect that somewhere in the world there lives a lady whom I have never seen, but who nevertheless has written a book that bears my name upon the title page. I wonder how often she was bored when she was writing it, and how frequently she wished that I would think more keenly or express myself more clearly. Somehow I hope that she will never tell.

CLAYTON HAMILTON

New York City: 1924.

# CONTENTS

# CONVERSATIONS ON
# CONTEMPORARY DRAMA

# CONVERSATIONS ON CONTEMPORARY DRAMA

## FIRST LECTURE

## THE CONTEMPORARY DRAMA

### FEBRUARY 11, 1924

ONLY a quarter of a century ago, when I was still an undergraduate in college, students were taught that there were three, or possibly four, great periods in the history of the drama,—the period of the Greeks at the time of Sophocles, the period of the Elizabethans at the time of Shakespeare, the period of the Spaniards at the time of Calderon (though our teachers were a little vague about this period, because few of them knew anything about it), and the period of the French at the time of Corneille, Racine, and Molière. At that time, toward the close of the eighteen-nineties, we were never told that the nineteenth century drama was worthy of studious consideration or that the contemporary drama was of any importance at all. Yet a great new drama had been launched into the world as long before as 1830, when the French romantics, led by Victor Hugo and Alexandre Dumas *père*, had revolutionized the art of the stage. This drama had been developed later by realistic writers like Emile Augier and Alexandre Dumas *fils,* and had been passed on to a great genius in Norway, the grim and tragic giant of the north. Henrik Ibsen had already attained his maturity and even passed the climax of his career in 1890; and his influence was making its impress in many other countries. A vivid new drama was launched in England by Sir Arthur Pinero in 1893 and was quickly developed by Mr. Henry Arthur Jones, Sir James Barrie, and Mr. Bernard Shaw. Germany came forward with the striking and influential plays of Hermann Sudermann and Gerhardt Hauptmann; the mysterious Maeterlinck appeared in Belgium; and important dramatic work was taken up and done in many other countries. Yet, when I was an undergraduate in college at the end of the eighteen-nineties, this contemporary drama was still considered unworthy of academic consideration, unworthy of serious study.

Of course, the only reason for so monstrous an anomaly was that the modern drama seemed too new and too near to our scholarly professors a quarter of a century ago. They were afraid it might not last, and they were not willing to run the risk of wasting any academic hours in a study of the possibly ephemeral. They did not know as much about the permanence of "Cyrano de Bergerac" in 1898, for instance, as we have learned in 1924. Time had taught them to be sure of Shakespeare; but they were not yet sure that Ibsen would outlast the nineteenth century. In this connection, I might remind you of an anecdote which some of you undoubtedly have heard. When Sir Arthur

Pinero, several years ago, was solemnly asked to formulate a definition of classic English comedy, he answered, "A classic English comedy is a successful farce by a writer who is dead."

I am very glad, however, that the academic attitude toward the contemporary drama has become more appreciative in the course of the last quarter of a century. Otherwise I should not be permitted to stand here, in a lecture hall of a great university, and talk to you, on nine successive Monday mornings, about plays that are actually being done in the theatre of to-day. But everybody nowadays—including even the most scholarly professors in our colleges—has at last become aware of the fact that we are living in the midst of a very wonderful period of dramatic creativity,—a period more vast and varied, more widespread and more versatile in its productiveness, than even those other great periods that I have mentioned,—the Greek, the Spanish, the Elizabethan, and the classic French. We are sure, at least, that the drama of the present period is great in quantity; and we have ample reason to believe that much of it is great in quality. At any rate, it is unquestionably worthy of serious study; and we enjoy the rare and great advantage of living in the midst of it and being able to watch it come into existence.

As students of the theatre, I think we should be rather proud of the fact that we are living in a period of such importance. A large number of centuries elapsed between the first two periods of greatness in the drama,—the period of Sophocles in the fifth century B.C. and the period of Shakespeare at the end of the sixteenth and the beginning of the seventeenth century A.D. Millions of people who were born and lived and died in that long interval of over two thousand years were not able to see any great play produced on a stage for the first time in the world. After the death of Molière, there was another interval of emptiness—not so long, indeed—a lapse of only one hundred and fifty to two hundred years—during which it was impossible for people anywhere to attend the first performance on the stage of any play of permanent importance. Yet, living in the present period, I have actually attended the world-première of several plays that seem destined to endure in the world's dramatic literature for centuries to come. In our own city of New York, which, since the war, has become the metropolis of the theatric world, we have frequent opportunities to observe the first production anywhere, or at least the first production in America, of plays that are immeasurably more important than any that were written in all the twenty centuries between Sophocles and Shakespeare. To remain obtuse to the contemporary drama, to refuse to regard it as worthy of most serious consideration, would be very much like living in Elizabethan London and neglecting to attend a performance of "Hamlet" or "Othello."

Yet the experience of living in a period of such dramatic productivity is so remarkable that it is a little difficult for us to appreciate the privilege. My own experience of theatre-going has covered a range of a third of a century. I began to attend the theatre regularly and systematically when I was about eight years old; and for nearly thirty-five years I have seen every play of any importance that has been produced in New York, not to mention plays that I have seen in other countries. That is not a long time, as history is measured: yet think how much has happened in those three decades and a half! When I began to go to the theatre, "Cyrano de Bergerac" had not been written. It is now established as an immortal masterpiece. When I began to go to the theatre, Sir James Barrie had not yet commenced to write plays. Mr. John Galsworthy had never been heard of; and I distinctly remember how queer I thought his name when I attended the first performance of his first play, "The Silver Box." Ibsen, of course, had nearly completed his life work when I was a boy, though I attended the first performances of his plays that were given in America; but think how much has been contributed to the drama of the world since the death of Ibsen! For instance, the entire literary movement that culminated in the establishment of the Irish National Theatre was launched less than thirty years ago; and it has given the world the deathless eloquence of J. M. Synge. Whenever we consider "The Playboy of the Western World," we feel as if it must always have belonged to dramatic literature; we feel, also, that the plays of Lord Dunsany must have existed for a long, long time; yet I was going to the theatre before these plays were written and, at the age of forty-two, I still persist in regarding myself as a member of "the younger generation." All of you are so familiar with the plays of J. M. Barrie that I will wager that it is a little difficult for you to realize that your grandparents never had the opportunity to see them. "Peter Pan" is so familiar to us nowadays that it is hard to imagine a world in which this fairy-tale did not exist. Great plays are now so frequent that their occurrence has become almost commonplace. I dare say that that is the reason why we spend so much energy worrying over the decadence of the stage and wondering what we can do to reform the theatre. People are constantly writing to the papers, lamenting the low estate to which the drama has declined and regretting the good old days; and I suppose that people uttered similar complaints in the period of Shakespeare and the period of Sophocles.

One reason why it is difficult for us to realize the importance of the contemporary drama is that it has not as yet been adequately analyzed, adequately appreciated, and adequately celebrated by dramatic criticism. Of course, in the history of any art, creation always precedes criticism, since criticism is merely an analysis of what has been created. The critic cannot do his work until he has something to criticize. His function is not to tell the dramatist how to make great plays, but to tell the public how great plays have been made. Consequently, criticism usually lags a generation or so behind creation. The great Greek dramatic critic, Aristotle, was not a contemporary of Euripides and

Sophocles; he came a generation later, and saw their work in retrospect. It takes about that long for a great movement in art to find its great critic; and I dare say that it may be twenty-five or fifty years before the real significance of our present-day creation in the drama is adequately analyzed and definitely estimated by commensurate dramatic criticism.

In this country at the present time we seem to be unfortunately lacking in dramatic criticism. In saying that, I have no intention of disparaging the reviewing of current plays as it is handled so entertainingly and oftentimes so charmingly by the writers for our metropolitan newspapers. I think that the literary standard of our newspaper reviewing is unusually high; but I don't think that much of this reviewing has anything to do with criticism. What Aristotle was endeavoring to do was very different from what Mr. Broun or Mr. Woollcott succeed in doing so delightfully. I perceive that I ought to tell you what criticism is; but I haven't time for that—it would take at least an hour—and, besides, if you really want to know, all you have to do is to read Matthew Arnold. He will tell you, among other things, that the purpose of criticism is to see the object as in itself it really is,—to see *the object,* mind you, and to write about the object,—not to write about oneself. A theatrical reviewer may say, "I saw a certain play last night and I did not like it at all"; but this statement has nothing to do with criticism if the reviewer goes on to say that the reason why he did not like the play is that his little boy had kept him awake

the night before with whooping-cough. When the
modern English drama was initiated in the eighteen-
nineties by Pinero and Jones, it was earnestly and seriously criticized by William Archer and Arthur Bing-
ham Walkley and George Bernard Shaw; and the
modern French drama has been excellently analyzed
throughout the course of its development, because the
French have a mind that is peculiarly adapted to the
purposes of criticism. But dramatic criticism is sorely
needed here and now, because the productive activity
of the contemporary theatre is so vast as to be bewilder-
ing. There has never been a period in the past when
there has been so much to appreciate, and so many
different kinds of things to appreciate, in the drama
of the moment; and it is difficult for the public, without critical guidance, to learn to appreciate at the same
time so many different kinds of creative endeavor.

It is an important point that the present period is
the first great period in history when the drama has
existed as an international art, when the drama has been
practiced in many different countries at the same time,
and when there has been an active interchange of plays
between the theatres of the different nations. This is
the first time in the history of the drama when there
has existed what I may call a standardized theatre,—
that is to say, when playhouses closely resembling
each other in their physical appointments have existed
simultaneously in several different countries inhabited
by different races speaking different languages. We
take this as a matter of course; but, if we will exercise

our historical memories, we shall observe that this condition has never existed before.

In the other great periods of the drama which I have mentioned, dramatic art was confined to a single nation and, it is scarcely an exaggeration to say, to a single city. All the plays that Aristotle saw were written by Athenians and for Athenians. The drama existed in Greece at that time, but it existed in no other country. It is true that certain plays that had been produced successfully in Athens were subsequently reproduced in other cities of Greece and Sicily; but, wherever they were done, the audience was always made up entirely of people of the same race, whose traditions were identical with those of the citizens of Athens. A Greek dramatist, when he wrote his play, was addressing a homogeneous audience of his own people; he could step upon the stage and actually look his entire public in the eyes. Thus, the task of the dramatist, in this particular regard, was much simpler in ancient Greece than is the task of the dramatist to-day. As our theatre is at present constituted, a play of more than ordinary merit is likely to be acted in several different countries and in several different languages; and the author can no longer look his public in the eyes. An emphatic instance of this international aspect of our modern drama was afforded to us a few months ago, when Eleanor Duse inaugurated her farewell tour of America with a performance of Ibsen's "The Lady from the Sea." Here was a play originally written in the Norwegian language, about Norwegian people, by a Norwegian author, who preferred to live in Germany. It was translated into the Italian language and acted by a company of Italian actors before an English-speaking audience in the metropolis of the new world. I must confess that I found the occasion a little incongruous,—especially when hundreds of enthusiasts who knew little about the play, and even less about the acting of Duse in her prime, stood up and cheered a performance which they could not understand. But the incongruity was less marked when, later in the same engagement, la Duse performed an Italian translation of Ibsen's "Ghosts." Here, I thought, the intention of the dramatist broke through the various barriers of race and language that had been erected between his authorship and the receptivity of the audience. But you will see that a much broader appeal— an appeal that transgresses the boundaries of nationality—is required of a modern dramatist like Ibsen than was required, in the Greek theatre, of a dramatist like Sophocles.

To pursue this point a little further, we may remind ourselves that, again, in the Elizabethan period, the drama was confined to a single country, and practically to a single city. One city was all that Shakespeare had to conquer. I suppose that Elizabethan London contained about two hundred thousand people. I am seldom exact as to figures; but, in any event, it was only a small city. When Shakespeare wrote a play, he knew that his audience was to be composed entirely of English people,—people of the same race, all speaking the same language, all living in the same community. His audience was a homogeneous one; and he never gave a moment's thought to the possibility of any market for his plays across the channel. Similarly, in the classic period of the French drama, dramatic art was once again confined to one country,—France. It was centralized in one city,—Paris; and, when Molière stepped forth upon the stage to act a comedy that he had written, he knew precisely the sort of people who would be sitting out in front.

But, at the present time, the problem of the dramatist is much more complicated. Although he writes primarily for an audience in his own country, it is inevitable, if he rises to a certain degree of eminence, that he will entertain a hope that his plays may be done elsewhere in the world. American playwrights, with one eye upon New York, have already developed a habit of writing with their other eye on London. The exportation of American plays, not only to England, but also to the various countries of continental Europe, is already more extensive than our general public realizes. Did you know, for instance, that Miss Margaret Mayo's farce called "Baby Mine," which has almost been forgotten in America, has held the stage in Spain for years and years as one of the most perennially popular of modern plays? Dozens of our American plays are now being done in several European languages; and, of course, it is not necessary to remind you that a great many European plays are being acted constantly in the American theatre, particularly in New York.

Now, whether or not an author, even under these conditions, can deliberately make an effort to address a world-wide audience is a question that is difficult to answer. Victorien Sardou, apparently, made this effort and succeeded; but he had Sarah Bernhardt to help him, and his plays were plays of plot instead of plays of character. Ibsen, although he lived for years in Italy and Germany, remained, throughout his long career, quite narrowly Norwegian in his outlook upon life. He never developed a cosmopolitan mind. He wrote about Norwegian people, leading circumscribed and stuffy lives in the provincial towns of Norway, and wrote his plays in the Norwegian language, a language understood by less than five million people in the entire world; yet these plays were ultimately translated into many other languages, and received with great interest by a world-wide audience. I wonder if Ibsen would have succeeded so well in other countries than his own if he had deliberately tried to be less local in his outlook upon life. I am afraid that, if he had said to himself, "I must try to interest not only the Teutonic, but also the Latin nations, I must imagine characters that will be equally interesting to Scandinavian and to Italian audiences," he might not have got anywhere at all. I am quite sure that Edmond Rostand never thought of a cosmopolitan audience when he was writing "Cyrano de Bergerac" for Coquelin. He was thinking only of the Parisian public; and yet his play—though utterly and absolutely French—captivated the entire world.

While apparently it would be very difficult, if not impossible, for a dramatist to attempt to address the whole world—except in the instance of a playwright so essentially mechanical and so professionally adroit as Victorien Sardou—yet we see that it has become customary, in the present period, for any play that is conspicuously successful in its own country to be shown in many other countries. Our leading dramatists are now expected to put into their work some quality that is not merely local, some quality that can transgress the boundaries of language and nationality and race. In this regard the contemporary drama has come to be a very catholic art. It requires a generality of understanding of human nature that was not absolutely necessary in the other great periods of the drama. Racine, for instance, who has always been regarded by the French as a dramatist of unquestionable greatness, is not usually so considered in the English-speaking countries. A finely civilized writer in a finely civilized period of a finely civilized nation, he knew nothing and cared nothing for the barbarians who lived across the channel and spoke the language of Shakespeare. Calderon, also, is almost utterly unknown outside of Spain; for Spain has always been and still remains comparatively out of touch with other countries,—an aloof and lonely nation that other people find it rather difficult to understand.

Now, since the drama has become, for the first time in history, an international art, we may discern one very obvious reason why a complete critical appreciation of the products of the present period cannot logically be expected for several years to come. The task for the dramatic critic at the present time is much too vast. A reviewer of the current theatre in New York has to see between two hundred and three hundred plays a year; yet, at the end of any season, he has not gathered sufficient material for any systematic study of the drama of to-day. So many worthy plays of so many different kinds are being written and produced in so many different countries that he can never hope to see them all or read them all, and, of course, he will never have an opportunity to codify them all and to deduce the laws of the contemporary drama as Aristotle deduced the laws of Greek tragedy from codifying the plays that he had seen.

In the other great periods, dramatic criticism was a comparatively easy task. Aristotle actually saw every play of permanent importance that had been written up to his time; and all these plays, as I have said, were written by Athenians and for Athenians. All of them were planned in accordance with the same technical method. This technical method was developed somewhat during the course of the three generations that extended from Æschylus through Sophocles to Euripides, but it was never basically altered. Aristotle's subject-matter was homogeneous; and it was a simple problem for a man of his clear intellect to deduce from a study of this homogeneous subject-matter the principles which governed it.

Similarly, it is not very difficult for scholarly critics

at the present time to deduce the laws of the Elizabethan drama. The great Elizabethan period endured for only half a century—from 1590 to 1640—and it is possible for a thorough scholar to read all of the extant plays that were written at that time. Again, these plays, as I have said, were written for the public of a single city, and present to the investigator a homogeneous group of documents. The technical method of the Elizabethan dramatists was scarcely altered from the days of Marlowe to the days of Shirley; and when we compare Shakespeare with Webster or Fletcher or Massinger or any of his other fellow-dramatists, we are comparing authors who approached the same problems in the same way and differed not in kind but only in degree. It is a much more difficult task for the critic to compare Pinero and Tchekoff and Maeterlinck and Sudermann and Brieux and Benavente,—to mention only a few of the leading dramatists of recent years; for these authors differ not only in degree but also in kind; they are approaching totally different problems in totally different ways.

In the period of Louis XIV, of France, it was a simple matter for dramatic critics to formulate the laws of French tragedy as practiced by Corneille and Racine, and not particularly difficult to formulate the laws of French comedy as practiced by Molière. But suppose that a dramatic critic should be asked to formulate the laws of the contemporary drama! It can't be done. Too many different kinds of technique are being prac-

ticed simultaneously, and the very faults of one playwright may become the virtues of another. The critic
may see a dozen different plays by leading dramatists,
and not one of them may show any resemblance to any
of the others, either in content or in form. And how is
he to find a formula that shall be equally applicable, let
us say, to "Hedda Gabler" and to "Peter Pan"?

The ideal dramatic critic, in the present period, would
be a rather extraordinary person. He would have to be
familiar with many languages, familiar with the life
of many different countries, familiar with the modes
of thought and feeling of many different nations;
and he would have to be so versatile in temperament
that he could shift the dominant mood of his mind,
from night to night, even from hour to hour, from one
nation to another. Some of us are so constituted that,
while we are primarily Americans, we have developed
through experience certain secondary selves. I am con-
scious, in my own case, although I am aware that I
am not particularly versatile, that it is very easy for
me to think and feel in French. The ideal spectator
in the theatre would be able to enjoy a play with his
French self, or his Italian self, or his Russian self, or
even—God help the man!—his German self, so that
his mood would be harmoniously suited to the mood
of the dramatist. But most spectators, and too many
reviewers even, are incapable of such a transforma-
tion. They see an Italian play with their American
eyes and say, "This is not interesting at all"; whereas,
if they could only borrow a pair of Italian eyes through

which to contemplate it, they might find it positively fascinating.

You may have gathered from this preliminary conversation something more than a hint that, in this brief course of nine lectures, I shall make no attempt to cover the entire field of the contemporary drama. All that I can possibly do is to talk of different particular topics within the limits of the general subject; and, in the choice of these particular topics, I shall gladly be guided by your wishes. I have not yet planned this course; and I should prefer to have you plan it for me. I dare say that you would like to have me talk about certain plays and playwrights that have come conspicuously before the public during the progress of the current theatre season in New York, and to remind you, now and then, of other plays and playwrights for the purpose of comparison and contrast. And since the outstanding success of the present season is Mr. Walton Hampden's revival—or reproduction, rather—of "Cyrano de Bergerac," I shall, with your permission, talk next time about Edmond Rostand.

# EDMOND ROSTAND

FEBRUARY 18, 1924

SOME of you may know that, as one of the Board of Directors of "Walter Hampden, Incorporated," I had a little to do with Mr. Hampden's decision to restore "Cyrano de Bergerac" to the American stage after a hiatus of twenty-two years. When this project was announced last spring, nearly every friend that Mr. Hampden had in the theatre business advised him not to court disaster with so hazardous an enterprise. They all said that "Cyrano" had been a good play in 1898 but that the public would not want to see it now, after a quarter of a century. Times had changed, and the piece would seem old-fashioned. To this Mr. Hampden answered that, however pertinent the argument might be to a realistic play that had been timely in 1898, it did not apply to "Cyrano," because this piece had not been timely in the year when it was first produced and was just as much out of date a quarter of a century ago as it is out of date to-day. He reasoned also that it would be a new play to all theatre-goers under thirty years of age; and he felt that its buoyant exuberance was a quality that would appeal particularly to the young people in the audience. He was warned by the wiseacres that the public of to-day did

not care for costume dramas and would not listen to
a play in verse; and the only way to answer that
warning was to produce the piece and find out. At
the first performance, on November first, the audience
stood up and cheered; and now, in its fourth month,
the piece is playing to twenty thousand dollars a week.

This morning, I shall review for you briefly the
career of the author of this entrancing play and shall
try to point out the most important qualities of his
work. It happens that I am only thirteen years younger
than Edmond Rostand. His first work was done
when I was in my early teens, which is, I think, the
very best time to become inoculated with the contagion
of this particular writer. "Cyrano de Bergerac" was
first produced and swept around the world when I was
sixteen years of age; and, in watching the later development of this poetic dramatist, I was able to see
everything that he did in the year in which he did it.
He died in 1918, at the early age of fifty. So, owing to
an accident of dates, I have witnessed his entire career
within the limits of my own lifetime. And yet, he
does not seem at all to be a contemporary figure. He
seems, rather, like some poet long ago and far away,
whose verses, like those of Horace, have endured for
centuries because their perfectness has shielded them
against decay.

Since this is supposed to be a course in the drama,
I ought to consider Rostand solely as a dramatist; but,
if I may be candid, I must confess at once that he has
always appealed to me mainly as a writer. Other men

have invented plays as good as his or better; but no
other man has ever shown a greater mastery of words.
I have always had an extraordinary fondness for him;
and, since I never met him in this world, I almost
wish that I believed in the existence of a heaven, so
that I might hope some day to sit at his feet and hear
him read aloud from his own writings. For it happened that this particular author was one of those who
taught me in my teens to love the loveliness of words—
a peculiar affection that I have not as yet been able to
outlive. I remember how, when I was sixteen, I used
to walk the streets repeating the verses of Rostand
over and over to myself. I find myself doing it to this
day. I do not know very much about the art of writing, because I have not had long enough to practice;
but I dare say that I have learned more about it from
this particular author than from almost any other—
except Dante, of course, and Sir Thomas Browne, and
Keats, and Robert Louis Stevenson. I know that
Rostand is a writer who appeals with particular
poignancy to anybody who has any love for setting
words together.

From the critical point of view, I am not sure that
Rostand is a great poet; but I know that he is a perfect
poet, and perfect poets are perhaps even rarer than
great poets. Rostand's literary qualities are, essentially, those of the minor poet. He is dainty, he is
delicate, he is witty and pretty, he is charming, he is
exquisite. Now, none of these adjectives could be
applied to the work of any of the great world-poets;

like Homer or Dante or Shakespeare or Goethe. We do not find in Rostand the magnitude, the majesty, the grandeur that we look for in the major poet. I do not think he ranks among the majors. But if he is merely a minor poet, he is, at least, the largest of the little poets of the world; and, as I said before, he is a perfect poet. By that I mean that he was incapable of writing badly,—that, during his entire life of half a century, he never wrote a bad line and never wrote a phrase that any other writer could possibly improve. Now, this is a virtue that we usually find only in the works of small poets, like Austin Dobson, who do little things, who attempt no big things, and whose product is rather limited. The large poet is likely to be care-less. He may write too quickly, like Lord Byron; or he may write rather shaggily, as Walt Whitman did. Whitman was gloriously eloquent when he was at his best; but, also, he could write very badly when he was at his worst. But a great poet may be allowed to write badly. He has so much to say that is of very great importance that, even when the expression is imperfect, the message is still welcome. But a minor poet who does little things must write perfectly. It is his only excuse for writing. Rostand began his career as a writer of minor verse. As time went on, his reach increased, but he never permitted it to exceed his grasp. He became a minor poet raised to the $n$th power; but he remained, essentially, a perfect maker of little things, rather than a vast and careless creator, like Walt Whitman.

The career of Rostand was curious in that it seemed to have no reference to his time. He was brought up in a period of realistic drama, when every one was aping Ibsen; but he took no interest in realism and cared nothing for the fashionable drama of the day. He was utterly unaffected by what was going on about him. All that he cared about was his own work, which had nothing to do with the work of anybody else. He had no predecessors—except Théodore de Banville; but this lovely lyric poet, of course, was not a dramatist. Furthermore, Rostand had no colleagues,—not even any imitators; and he has brought forth no successors. His work was unique; and when he died, it ceased,—a perfect and completed thing. As Jonson said of Shakespeare,—"He was not of an age, but for all time." A thousand years from now, if his work is read by Ph.D.'s, it will be impossible from internal evidence to assign it to a century. I don't think that any Ph.D. will argue from internal evidence that the plays of Rostand were written in the nineteenth century, or in the twentieth, or in the eighteenth; and yet they will not seem to have been written in the period of Racine and Molière. Perhaps the surest way to conquer death is to live and work in utter scorn of time.

This poet had a very happy life. He was an aristocrat, he was wealthy, he was a gentleman of leisure. He enjoyed all of those advantages which are popularly regarded as disadvantages to a literary artist. I wonder who it was that started the superstition that a poet must learn in sorrow what he sings in song and that the best way to get good work out of a writer is to starve him in a garret. I dare say it must have been some publisher or theatre manager. The only handicap to Rostand's career was his delicate physical condition, his chronic ill-health. But he never talked about it. His physical disability was never advertised, like that of Robert Louis Stevenson. Perhaps he might have worked more rapidly if he had been a stronger man; but time meant nothing to him; he had plenty of money, and he could afford to spend ten years in writing "Chantecler."

He was born in Marseilles, in 1868—though the date doesn't matter in the least. He came of a distinguished family. His father, a man of wealth and fine position, was a poet; and his uncle, a noted economist, was also a poet. He was brought up in an atmosphere of luxury and leisure and was accustomed to culture from his earliest years. He wrote verses throughout his childhood and his teens. Then he went up to Paris to acquire a formal education. He studied law at the Lycée Stanislas, which was of course a gentlemanly thing to do, and was admitted to the bar; but he never wasted any time in practicing law. He did not have to earn his living; and it was more important for him to practice the patterning of consonants and vowels. At an early age—twenty-one, I think—he married Rosemonde Gérard,—an excellent lyric poet and a granddaughter of a Marshal of France. Their son, Maurice, is now a very promising

poet and playwright. Rostand's first volume was a
collection of little lyrics, called "Les Musardises."
This title means, in English, "Wastes of Time"; but
though the poems perhaps are not important, they are
exquisite and charming, and each is in itself a perfect
thing. His earliest plays were produced in his twenties; and the first of all, "Les Romanesques," was immediately accepted by the Comédie Française. He
did not have to wait long years for recognition, and
he was successful from the very start. "Cyrano de
Bergerac" was produced when he was only twenty-
nine. It is interesting to note that this is the most
successful play that has ever been produced at any
time in the history of the drama. Over half a million
copies of the original French text have been sold
throughout the world; and this number, of course,
takes no account of translations into other languages.
The play has been acted in nearly every country where
a theatre exists, and has always been successful every-
where. It was a great misfortune that this perfect
workman died at the early age of fifty. His constitu-
tion, as I have said, was always frail; and he died
in 1918, of influenza and pneumonia, after an illness
of only a few days. In a sense, however, his life work
was completed; because I think whatever he might
have written in the future would have been similar in
character and quality to what he had written in the
past. We should have had more of Rostand, but not
a different Rostand. It was not in him to change the
nature of his endeavor, as Ibsen changed the quality

and purpose of his work when he was over fifty.
Rostand left behind him a very beautiful play, "La
Dernière Nuit de Don Juan." Since he had to die, I
am very glad that he lived long enough to see the flag
of France flying on the ramparts of the Rhine.

Now I shall take up, one by one, his half a dozen
plays and say a few words about each of them in turn.

His first play, "Les Romanesques," was produced
in 1894, when the author was twenty-six years old.
The title means, in English, "The Story-Book People";
and the general stage direction reads as follows,—
"The action happens wherever you wish, provided that
the costumes are pretty." A rather good beginning,—
don't you think? When the curtain rises, we find
ourselves in a garden divided into two by a wall down
the center of the stage. On the top of the wall, a very
young man is sitting. On the other side of the wall,
a very young girl is standing on a bench. They look
a little like figurines in Dresden China. A large book
is held open in the young man's lap, and he is reading
aloud. He is reading a lyric love scene from an old
romantic play, called "Romeo and Juliet." We soon
find out that these young people are very romantic,
that they are in love with each other, and that the only
thing that thwarts their love is the prosaic fact that
their fathers are next door neighbors and fast friends.
How terrible it is that there should be nothing to keep
them apart! So their fathers, knowing this, have to
pretend to quarrel with each other. When their
fathers apparently fall out, the young lovers are de-

lighted.  It would now be logical for them to elope;
so, with the aid of a sympathetic character called Straforel, they arrange to run away.  Straforel is a pro-
fessional caterer in elopements.  He will get up any
kind of elopement that you wish,—first class, or second
class, or third class.  You may elope without a carriage, or you may have a carriage with one horse, or
two horses, *et cetera,* according to your tastes.  The
young people have a perfectly delightful time arrang-
ing an elopement with all the trimmings.  Then, unfortunately, they make the tragic discovery that their
fathers are not enemies at all; and, of course, there is
nothing they can do but part forever.  How could they
possibly go on loving each other without an impedi-
ment?

That is an outline of the first act; and, if I had the
time to review the three acts of "Les Romanesques," I
don't think I could give you any better idea of the
composition.  It is as light as thistledown.  The only
possible reason for writing such a piece would be the
fun of writing it with faultless art; for perfect literary
craftsmanship is its own excuse for being.  I have
said that Rostand had no predecessors; but if, per-
chance, the planet Venus twinkled when "Les Romanesques" was written, it may have been because
Alfred de Musset was up there, smiling, and throwing
little sidelong glances down with understanding eyes.

Rostand's next undertaking was a little more sub-
stantial, for he was growing more mature.  He was

twenty-seven years old when Sarah Bernhardt produced "La Princesse Lointaine" in 1895. I suppose you are familiar with the legend of Rudel and the lady of Tripoli,—at least from Browning's poem. The troubadour, Rudel, has fallen profoundly in love, by hearsay, with the lady Mélissinde, a princess of the East, who is reputed to be the most beautiful woman in the world. Anybody, according to Rudel, can fall in love with a woman who is thrust upon him by propinquity,—whom he can see and listen to and touch,— but it takes a poet to fall in love with a woman he has never seen; and, while he is about it, he might just as well fall in love with the most beautiful woman in the world. But Rudel falls very ill; and, when he is sick nigh unto death, he thinks that he would like to see the lady of his love before he dies. So he organizes an expedition to sail for Tripoli; and they start out in a gorgeous caravel. He takes along with him many other knights and troubadours and gentlemen,—among them his dearest friend, Bertrand D'Allamanon. After many hardships, they come in sight of land. By that time, Rudel is so ill that he begs his friend, Bertrand, to go ashore and call upon the princess and convey to her his own poetic messages of love. Now, the lady of Tripoli had heard of the troubadour Rudel and had read the poems he had written to her. When his ship appears, she is naturally interested; and when Bertrand comes ashore, looking very young and very handsome, she at once assumes that he is the troubadour,—par-

ticularly since, at the first sight of her, he drops to his
knees and recites a set of verses that Rudel had written to her overseas.   So she falls in love with him at
once, assuming that he is Rudel; and Bertrand falls in
love with her.   Here, then, we have a strong dramatic
situation; for Bertrand, acting as an emissary of his
best friend, has fallen in love with the lady that his
best friend has long adored, while his best friend is
lying at the point of death.   It is a situation that calls
for an heroic exercise of the obsolescent poetry of
gentlemanliness.   This play has nothing to do with
the nineteenth century and still less with the twentieth.
It has nothing to do with anything that seems important to most people at the present time.   But it has
picturesqueness, it has charm, it has the forlorn loveliness of longing for ideals long ago and far away.

It contains one song of which I am particularly
fond,—the song of the troubadour Rudel to his princess far away; and, because I like this song, I am going
to read it to you,—for love of lovely words.   It may
be that some of you do not understand the French
language.   I am sorry for you if you don't; but, in
this case, it does not matter at all.   The value of this
song is in its sound.   Its meaning is comparatively
immaterial; but, if you insist on knowing what it
means, the general sense of it is that anybody can love
a light-haired girl or a dark-haired girl or a red-haired
girl if she is around all the time, but it takes a poet to
love a girl he has never seen.   But this is how it
sounds:

C'est chose bien commune
De soupirer pour une
Blonde, châtaine ou brune
   Maîtresse,
Lorsque brune, châtaine,
Ou blonde, on l'a sans peine.
—Moi, j'aime la lointaine
   Princesse!

C'est chose bien peu belle
D'être longtemps fidèle,
Lorsqu'on peut baiser d'Elle,
   La traine,
Lorsque parfois on presse
Une main, qui se laisse ⸱ ⸱ ⸱
Moi, j'aime la Princesse
   Lointaine!

Car c'est chose suprême
D'aimer sans qu'on vous aime,
D'aimer toujours, quand même,
   Sans cesse,
D'une amour incertaine,
Plus noble d'être vaine ⸱ ⸱ ⸱
Et j'aime la lointaine
   Princesse!

Car c'est chose divîne,
D'aimer lorsqu'on devine,
Rêve, invente, imagine
   A peine ⸱ ⸱ ⸱
Le seul rêve intéresse,
Vivre sans rêve, qu'est-ce?
Et j'aime la Princesse
   Lointaine!

Rostand's next piece of work was "La Samaritaine,"
—"The Woman of Samaria,"—which was produced
by Sarah Bernhardt in 1897. If the lyricism of "La
Princesse Lointaine" is like the music of harps in the
air, the graver music of "La Samaritaine" is like the

throbbing of some vast cathedral organ that shakes you into sanctity. The author did not call this piece "a play in three acts"; he called it "a sermon in three pictures." It is a very simple thing. The leading figures are Jesus and the woman of Samaria. In the first act, the woman of Samaria encounters Jesus at a wayside well and is converted to become one of His followers. In the second act, she goes forth and gathers a large crowd to listen to Him. And, in the third act, Jesus talks to the crowd that she has gathered. "La Samaritaine" seems to me one of the most beautiful and one of the most effective presentations of the character of Jesus that have been written in any literature. The part of Jesus is a long part in the play; but the character is never made to say anything whatever that is not recorded in at least one of the four gospels. The selected sayings are assembled with such exquisite art and the part is written with such serene poetic beauty that I sincerely think that the presentation of the character of Jesus in "La Samaritaine" is more effective than the presentation of the same character in the French translations of the Bible. Of course, "La Samaritaine" was not intended as a theatrical play; it was prepared for special performances at Eastertide. From the poetic point of view, however, it is perhaps the loftiest of Rostand's compositions; for not elsewhere has he risen to that serene simplicity which, in this instance, was required of him by his lofty theme.

Not many years ago, "La Samaritaine" was presented in this country by Sarah Bernhardt; and, at that time, it was taken to the city of Philadelphia. The performance was forbidden by the police, and the actors were threatened with arrest. The city of Philadelphia, in those days, was noted for its saloons, its gambling halls, its prize-fights, and the open-armed hospitality of its houses of ill-fame; but it was shocked at the idea of a public exhibition of a sermon on the stage. Of course, "La Samaritaine" was not written for an uncivilized public. It was written for the citizens of France.

It was as a result of these achievements that Rostand received an opportunity to write "Cyrano de Bergerac." I speak of it in terms of opportunity; because this play would never have been undertaken had it not been for the advice and assistance and collaboration of a great actor, the late Constant Coquelin. Coquelin, the greatest comedian of his time and one of the great comedians of all time, perceived that Rostand had the necessary talent for writing an heroic comedy: so he sent for the young poet and said to him, "I have come to that point in my career when I would like to have a great acting part, as great an acting part as Hamlet, a part that will permit me in a single evening to do all that I can do. The only trouble is that I can do nearly everything. I am primarily a comedian, and of course you must give me an opportunity to play all kinds of comedy,—humorous, witty, satirical, extravagant, grotesque, buffoon. But I am also a poetic actor. I have a great voice, and I can read. I can even make love; and then, too, I am one of the few comedians who can die." So they sought for a part that would permit this versatile actor to do everything in his repertoire,—to make love, to be poetical, to be gallant, to fight a duel, to play a battle scene, to die, and every now and then to chant bravura passages in that incomparable voice of his; and they hit upon the historical character of Cyrano de Bergerac, who had actually lived in the days of Molière.

The point that interested Rostand particularly was that Cyrano had an enormous nose which gave him a grotesque appearance, while at the same time he had the soul of a poet. The idea of a man who was very beautiful inside and not at all beautiful on the outside was a fascinating idea to Rostand, because it seemed to him typical of life at large. All of us, I think, have some beauty hidden inside of us that is not visible to the eyes of those who look upon us from the outside.

The play was worked out in constant consultation with Coquelin; and this collaboration, doubtless, helped to make it the perfect piece of theatrical craftsmanship that it unquestionably is. I know of other plays that may be greater, but I know of none more perfectly planned or more perfectly written. If a messenger should suddenly descend from Mars and ask me to explain to him in a single evening what the theatre meant on earth, I think that I should take him to a performance of "Cyrano de Bergerac."

When this play was first produced at the Théâtre de la Porte Saint-Martin on the twenty-eighth of December, 1897, it took Paris by storm. I was in this country at that time; and I remember that, when the first rumors came overseas, within a week or two, they were to the effect that a comparatively unknown poet, only twenty-nine years of age, had actually written the greatest play in the history of the world. I do not think that "Cyrano" is that, because I have seen "Othello" and I have seen "The Trojan Women." But no other play in history has been so immediately and so enormously successful in every country of the world. I think the reason for this is that the play has certain qualities which are exceedingly contagious to the audience and which everybody in the audience desires to have stimulated within himself. It has beauty, it has gallantry, it has love, it has satire, it has bravery, it has humor, it has pathos. And I think that the average auditor, catching these qualities by contagion, finds it very easy to identify himself with Cyrano de Bergerac and to experience vicariously, within himself, what is shown upon the stage. Cyrano does and says what all of us would like to do and say, what all of us in our dreams have always done and said. And his passion for the beautiful gesture is so gallant and so glorious and so young! Those critics who would have us think that literature, to be impressive, must be doleful might dismiss "Cyrano de Bergerac" as immature; but I think that youth perhaps is more important than maturity.

Of course, if we should take the fable very seriously, I am afraid that we could not deny that Cyrano is guilty of the sin, or I might even call it the crime, of self-sacrifice. I call self-sacrifice a crime; for, if we have learned anything at all in the present stage of the universe, we have learned that the primary object of life is not self-sacrifice but self-fulfillment. It is the duty of every individual in the world to contribute to the general furtherance of the evolution of the universe by developing himself to the utmost possible degree to which that self of his may be developed; and anybody who sacrifices himself, and by such spiritual suicide stints the general cause of evolution, is obviously guilty of a crime,—one of the most regrettable crimes in the world. Now, Cyrano is guilty of the crime of self-sacrifice. He gives up his own love as hopeless, and conspires to marry off the lady that he loves to an empty-headed gallant with a pretty face, thereby consigning her to a life of misery, in order that he himself may enjoy the luxurious agony of his gesture of unselfishness. With my philosophic mind, I think that that is a dastardly thing to do; yet Cyrano is applauded in the theatre for this very deed, and I must admit that I applaud him with the rest. Why do we applaud self-sacrifice? It is because our emotions have evolved more slowly than our intelligence. For two thousand years, self-sacrifice has been preached throughout the occidental world as a virtue; it has even been recommended as a duty; and though, with our intellects, we may know better and think otherwise, we cannot rescue our emotions from that ancestral heritage of superstition.

I should like to add that I never fully realized the perfect craftsmanship of "Cyrano de Bergerac" until I was associated with Mr. Walter Hampden in the rehearsals of the current reproduction. We had the advantage of working with a great translation. "Great" is an adjective that I use very sparingly; but I think that it may justly be applied to Mr. Brian Hooker's new version of "Cyrano" in English verse. Professor Brander Matthews put the matter perfectly when he said, "It is utterly impossible to translate 'Cyrano de Bergerac' into English verse; and Brian Hooker has done it." Mr. Hooker followed the original text speech for speech and line for line; he omitted nothing; and, when we had the play in rehearsal, we saw that it was at least twenty minutes too long. For the convenience of prospective patrons who would have to catch the last train to Montclair or New Rochelle, we had to take out lines here and there, cheating a little where we hoped the cheat would not be noticed, in order to save that twenty minutes; but it was a heart-breaking task, as if a surgeon had been called upon to amputate a little finger of his best beloved child. We discovered that the entire text was woven like a piece of tapestry; and, when we tried to cut out a little speech, we not only made a hole in the fabric, but everything around the hole began to unravel. At the next rehearsal, I could seldom hear anything except the lines we had left out. I have been through the rehearsals of many plays, including half a dozen of my own; and "Cyrano" is the only play that seemed to bleed wherever it was cut.

Rostand's next play, "L'Aiglon," was also intended, at the outset, as a vehicle for Coquelin. The great comedian had always wanted to play a Napoleonic grenadier,—a grouchy old soldier with a great moustache; and the poet started out from a central conception of the character of Flambeau. But before long the dramatist encountered a great difficulty. He came to Coquelin and said, "Your character of the grumpy old grenadier is coming along all right; but the trouble is with Napoleon. As soon as he steps upon the stage, nobody will look at anybody else, not even at you." Of course that has always been the difficulty in any play in which Napoleon has figured. The reason is that Napoleon himself was the best theatricist in history and one of the best dramatists. All you have to do to appreciate that quality of his is to go to his tomb and read the inscription around it, which was written by himself. I am neither a soldier nor a statesman and I haven't any critical opinion of Napoleon's prowess in either of those capacities; but I know a prose sentence when I hear one, and I insist upon saluting a man who could write an epitaph like this: "Je désire que mes cendres reposent sur les bords de la Seine, au milieu de ce peuple français que j'ai tant aimé." So Coquelin said to Rostand, "The only thing to do is to kill the Emperor off and set your play after he is dead. If you lay your scene after the

death of Napoleon, I, the old soldier, will be loyal
to his memory."

So Rostand set to work a second time, setting the
play in the period of Napoleon's insignificant little son.
He conceived a sort of "Hamlet,"—a play about a
young man overcome with the burden of circumstances
inherited from his father and feeling himself unable
to cope with them. But, after a time, the poet came
to Coquelin again and said: "It is worse than ever
now; nobody will look at you; because that frail little
boy in his white uniform is such an appealing figure
that, whenever he comes upon the stage, everybody's
heart goes out to him." So Coquelin, still longing to
play his grouchy old soldier with the great moustache,
regretfully conceded that the project was impossible.
"Take the piece to Sarah," he said, "she's just played
Hamlet and wants to do another boy."

The great thing about "L'Aiglon" is the complete-
ness with which it quintessentializes the Napoleonic
period. When people like Mr. H. G. Wells discover
history, they usually like to throw out their chests and
hurl mud at Napoleon. The gesture makes them feel
important. But men like Rostand have written poems
about Napoleon; and I don't think that any one will
ever write a poem about Mr. H. G. Wells. The brief-
est way for me to indicate to you the spirit of
"L'Aiglon" is merely to read you the dedication of the
play. It is written in a single sentence of prose; but
if you have ears to hear, this sentence will march into
your heart like an army with banners: "A mon fils

Maurice, et à la mémoire de son héroïque arrière-grand-père Maurice, comte Gérard, Maréchal de France."

I find, to my regret, that I have left myself no time for an adequate discussion of Rostand's next and final play, "Chantecler." The author took ten years to write this piece; and it is not a thing to be disposed of in a moment. "Chantecler," like "Cyrano," was written for Coquelin. By his intimate friends, the great actor was always called "Coq"; and it happened that that diminutive coincided with the French word for rooster. It was from this suggestion that Rostand conceived his fantastic idea of the magnified barnyard. The cock, as you know, is the symbol of France; and it was quite natural to imagine Coquelin playing a rooster, which would be at once a symbol of France, and a symbol of the artist, and a symbol of the human soul. "Chantecler" failed in the theatre, because Coquelin died before it was produced, and Guitry, though an admirable actor, was not equal to the leading part. But I fear that it might have failed anyway, because it was too intricately clever. The author devoted too much time to the task of writing it; and the workmanship is so brilliant and so amazing that one can hardly see the forest for the trees.

And now, before I let you go, I want to allow Rostand himself to do the last of the talking; and, to this end, I shall close by reading you a sonnet that he wrote while the Huns were expressing themselves by bombarding the Cathedral of Rheims. It seems to me the

finest of the poems inspired by the war, because it is
the most civilized; and, though I doubt if Mr. Edward
Bok would pay me a prize of fifty thousand dollars for
the suggestion, I think that the peace of the world
might be assured if every child in every school of Germany could be required to learn this sonnet by heart
and to recite it once a day for the next twenty-five
years. There is no hate in the poem, no anger, not
even any indignation; there is nothing but a smiling
pity.

### LA CATHÉDRALE

Ils n'ont fait que la rendre un peu plus immortelle.
   L'Œuvre ne périt pas, que mutile un gredin.
   Demande à Phidias et demande à Rodin
Si, devant ses morceaux, on ne dit plus: "C'est Elle!"

La Forteresse meurt quand on la démantèle,
   Mais le Temple, brisé, vit plus noble; et soudain
   Les yeux, se souvenant du toit avec dédain,
Préfèrent voir le ciel dans la pierre en dentelle.

Rendons grace—attendu qu'il nous manquait encor
D'avoir ce qu'ont les Grecs sur la colline d'or:
   Le Symbole du Beau consacré par l'insulte!—
Rendons grace aux pointeurs du stupide canon,
   Puisque de leur adresse allemande il résulte
Une Honte pour eux, pour nous un Parthénon.

# GEORGE BERNARD SHAW

### FEBRUARY 25, 1924

BECAUSE of the conspicuous success of "Saint Joan" at the Garrick Theatre, it has been suggested that I talk to you this morning about the work of Mr. Bernard Shaw.

For some reason or other, I missed the first performance of this latest play of his; and, since I have grown of late a little lazy in my theatre-going, I did not get around to it until last week, when it became desirable that I should see it if I were to talk about it this morning. I say "desirable"; but I do not say "necessary." I am quite sure that I could have talked about "Saint Joan" without having seen it; for the mind of Mr. Shaw is thoroughly consistent, and anybody who knows his mind can always predict in advance exactly what he is going to say about a particular subject. In the early days of August, 1914, I predicted that Mr. Shaw would argue that England was just as wrong in defending the neutrality of Belgium as Germany was in violating it; and, surely enough, Mr. Shaw came forward with such a statement within a week or two. He wasn't going to let anybody get away with the old-fashioned idea that right is right and wrong is wrong.

Although I did not see "Saint Joan" until last Tuesday night, I knew in advance what Mr. Shaw would think of Joan of Arc. I knew the sort of play that he would write on this subject; and for that reason I did not believe any of the reviews of "Saint Joan" that I had read. And, though it is more blessed to praise than to condemn, I hope that you will not be misled by the laudatory tone of these reviews. "Saint Joan" is a poor play. It is almost unpardonably poor; for it would seem that any dramatist endowed with such remarkable ability as Mr. Shaw has frequently exhibited on past occasions ought to have been able to make a more impressive thing out of a dramatization of the character of one of the most appealing figures in all history. I was not surprised to find the composition tedious, for Mr. Shaw has grown garrulous in recent years; but I was a little surprised to find that long passages of it were dull, and I was actually astonished to discover that the piece never reached a point which aroused the spectator to that emotional enthusiasm and spiritual elevation which, obviously, are inherent in the theme. Mr. Shaw gave himself plenty of time. The play occupies nearly three hours and a half. And it seems to me a little difficult to imagine how any dramatist of notable ability could talk three hours and a half about Joan of Arc, of all people, without ever calling tears into the eyes. I don't mean tears of sadness; I mean tears of enthusiasm. There is nothing more moving in the world than the spectacle of many people paying tribute to one. Suppose there is a parade upon the avenue and that some hero [if only a hero of the moment] rides down the street on horseback. Of course the hero ought to look heroic: he should have the proper make-up for the part, as General Pershing has, for instance. Then, when the crowd cheers, a lump will gather in your throat. Now, there is in all history no more appealing figure than the Maid of France. Multitudes have paid tribute to her, throughout uncounted generations. She incorporates, and has incorporated for six hundred years, the soul of a nation, the most gallant nation in the world. It is inconceivable that she could ride down the street on horseback without bringing tears to the eyes. But, at Mr. Shaw's play, you sit and listen to her for three hours and never even care.

Of course this paradox arises from the analytic method of Mr. Shaw. Instead of writing history, he has written a criticism of history. Instead of writing biography, he has written a criticism of biography. Instead of creating a character, he has written a criticism of the character. He has written a treatise on Joan of Arc instead of writing Joan of Arc.

When you saw this play, I wonder if you realized what a bad part Mr. Shaw has written for his leading actress. Here is the central part in an historical drama, the title part of the play, a part supposed to represent one of the greatest figures in all history: and what is the actress asked to do?—Talk; and nothing else. I watched the part very carefully; and I think that I am right in saying that, during the entire evening of three hours and a half, the actress impersonating Joan of Arc is given only one piece of stage business to do. In the trial scene, she is allowed to read a paper that she has signed under duress and to tear it to pieces. Once or twice, during the course of the play, she kneels down and gets up again. Otherwise, she is given nothing whatever to do but stand around and read lines. Miss Winifred Lenihan, who plays the part at the Garrick Theatre, complains that many of these lines are out of character. She says that just as she is about to realize within her own imagination the mood of Joan of Arc and to communicate it by contagion to the audience, Mr. Shaw makes her say something which disrupts the mood and shatters the illusion. This is sound criticism. But, even if many of the lines were not annoyingly out of character, it would be difficult for any actress to suggest the Maid of Orléans without the aid of any action whatsoever. For the historical Joan of Arc led a very active life. She did things; and she got things done. Her public career lasted only about a year, and she was a very, very busy person in the time allotted to her. She was not a talkative person; she was not a reflective person; she was not an analytic person. She was not interested in reasons but solely in results. The only right way to represent her on the stage would be to show her doing something all the time. She should have at least as much to do as Rostand's gallant hero, Cyrano de Bergerac. Cyrano does a good deal of talking, but, through it all, he is always doing something.

In "Saint Joan" we are told that, off-stage and between scenes, the heroine has accomplished this or that; but we do not see her accomplish it. We are told that she has won a battle here or there; but we are never taken to the battle. We are told that she has been captured by the enemy; but we do not see her captured. Whenever in history she did anything that was dramatic, that something is left off the stage. We are allowed to come along a week afterward and listen to Mr. Shaw while he delivers a lecture about it. Is that a great way to dramatize a great historic theme? I do not think so.

Nobody else in the play has anything to do but talk; yet the piece is supposed to represent a savage century of history when people acted first and thought afterwards, if ever. They did not sit around and argue or philosophize. They sprang to horse and went out and cut each other's throats. Imagine what Shakespeare would have done with such a period. The stage would have been noisy with alarums and excursions, the hurrying hither and thither of armed men. There would have been battle scenes, as in "Henry V": "Once more into the breach!" . . . There would have been something to get enthusiastic about. Yet, at Mr. Shaw's play, you sit unmoved for three hours and a half and are not even made to care about France.

Many of the conversations are interesting in their

way.  Of course, they are studded with anachronisms:
and I do not mean anachronisms of fact, I mean anachronisms of idea: but it is rather amusing to hear
a fifteenth century personage uttering ideas that did
not become current in the world until after 1918.  The
Bishop of Beauvais is a very able conversationalist: he
is Mr. Shaw talking about a period of history.  The
inquisitor, however, is too loquacious to be interesting
after the first three or four minutes of his lengthy
lecture.  The trial scene, which is the one scene the
audience has been waiting for and really wants to see,
is ruined by the interminable talk of the inquisitor before Joan is brought upon the stage.  The auditors are
so tired of the trial by that time that they no longer care
whether she is burned or not.  Then, after the play is
over, the author appends an epilogue, in which he
discusses his historical material again.  He now writes
a criticism of what he has already written,—a criticism
of a criticism.

I am informed in print by my friend and colleague,
Mr. Heywood Broun, that "Saint Joan" is the finest
play that has been written in the English language
within the limits of his memory.  I don't know how
far back his memory extends, nor when he lost it;
but I should think it ought to go back to "Mid-Chan-
nel" and "The Thunderbolt," "A Kiss for Cinderella"
and "What Every Woman Knows," "Strife," "The
Playboy of the Western World," "The Gods of the
Mountain," or at least to "Anna Christie" and "Beyond
the Horizon."  If "Saint Joan" is a finer play than

any of these, I shall have to shoot myself before next Monday morning; for it would be presumptuous of me to appear before you once again to talk to you about the drama.

"Saint Joan" was immediately successful at the box-office. It was praised in superlative terms by most of the reviewers. The public goes to see it, is bored, and is afraid to say so. It is a popular play, because there is nothing more potent in the theatre than fashion. I received a letter a few months ago from Mr. Henry Arthur Jones, who is now seventy-two years old, in which he said that more and more as time went on he became convinced that vogue counted more than anything else for momentary success in the theatre. Mr. Bernard Shaw became the fashion a few years ago,—after he had ceased to write good plays. His name is very valuable in the theatre, because the American public is more impressed by a successful name than by an anonymous work of worthy art. As an illustration of this fact, you might look any month at the cover of the "Cosmopolitan Magazine."

But let us not forget that Mr. Shaw wrote "Candida," and several other worthy plays, before he became a fashionable dramatist with a successful name. Let us now review his career and remind ourselves of the dominant characteristics of his mind.

Mr. Shaw was born in 1856 and is now sixty-eight years old, or thereabouts. He was born in Dublin of a middle-class Protestant family. His father, a minor government official, was an unsuccessful man. Mr.

Shaw's mother, however, was a woman of unusual ability,—a skilled musician, who had also a keen knowledge of the other arts. She became a teacher of music and thereby helped to support her husband and her son. Mr. Shaw went to school in the ordinary way; but he has said that his years in school were the most utterly wasted of his life. In his teens, he went to work in the office of a land agent and tried to help support his mother. Upon the death of his father, Mr. Shaw's mother moved to London; and her son followed her at the age of twenty.

During the next nine years, from the age of twenty to the age of twenty-nine, Mr. Shaw was exceedingly poor. He devoted himself to literary work; and, since he had no money, he was obliged to live on a small allowance from his mother. He wrote assiduously and constantly for nine years; and, during this total period, he tells us that he earned exactly six pounds by the product of his pen. Thirty dollars in nine years! This period had a strong effect upon the development of his habits and his tastes. Largely because of his extreme poverty, he adopted in his early twenties an exceedingly abstemious routine of life; and, since he is the sort of man who intellectualizes his own habits into principles, he has preached abstemiousness ever since. He does not eat meat, he does not smoke tobacco, he does not drink liquor; and he gets up early in the morning. These habits, as I say, he has retained throughout his years of affluence; and, transmuting them to principles, he would impose them upon others. He says that everybody ought to live on lettuce and nuts and early morning air. Everybody ought to go without meat, without drink, without tobacco. When people protest against such abnormality, Mr. Shaw argues that he himself is a thoroughly normal person and that everybody else is abnormal.

During his twenties, Mr. Shaw wrote three clever novels which attracted no attention at the time, though in later years they were republished with some degree of success; but he did not seem to be getting anywhere. But at the age of twenty-nine a great change came in his career. He met Mr. William Archer. At that time Mr. William Archer was the foremost dramatic critic in the English language. He had discovered Ibsen. He had introduced Ibsen's plays to English readers. It was Mr. Archer who suggested to Mr. Shaw that, instead of writing novels that nobody wanted to read, he should seek a regular job as a critic for some periodical. It happened that Mr. Shaw's mind was particularly suited to the task of criticism; and he soon became a very able critical reviewer. For several years he served on the staff of the "Saturday Review," writing not only dramatic criticism but also criticism of music and painting. He knew a great deal about music, which he had learned from his mother; he knew something about painting; he knew a little about the drama; and he wrote very cleverly about all three. As a dramatic critic he was not so philosophical as Mr. Archer nor so unprejudiced, not so sound nor so safely to be depended on; but he was much more brilliant and more keen.

It was Mr. Archer, also, who suggested that Mr. Shaw should try his hand at a play. The two critics collaborated, and started to write a piece called "Widowers' Houses"; but they laid it aside for some reason or other when they had written only an act, and Mr. Archer ultimately lost interest in it. Subsequently, however, Mr. Shaw finished it up alone; and "Widowers' Houses" became the first of his dramatic compositions. Soon afterward he wrote "The Philanderer" and "Mrs. Warren's Profession." In the middle of his thirties, he was still a dramatic critic trying to write plays; and his plays, interesting as they were, were obviously written by a critic.

I have said already that his mind has not changed since his twenties, although of course it has developed. He began life as a critic. He wrote his early plays as a critic. And he is still writing plays as a critic. He is always criticizing his subject-matter; and his art is a "criticism of life" in a sense much narrower than that intended by Matthew Arnold when he coined that famous phrase.

Mr. Shaw's early plays were produced only privately, when they were produced at all; and again he did not seem to be getting anywhere. Then he conceived a clever idea and did what, at the time, was an extraordinary thing. He decided to publish his plays, accompanied by critical prefaces which should assure the public that his plays were masterpieces. If Mr. Shaw had invented nothing else, he would deserve a place in history as the inventor of the habit of self-advertising which has become so fashionable among the writers of the present day. At the time when Mr. Shaw conceived this clever idea, the publication of English plays was utterly uncustomary; indeed, for a long time, because of defective copyright legislation, it had been impossible for English authors to publish their plays without losing control of the acting rights. This situation was remedied at the outset of the eighteen-nineties; but, by continuance of an established custom, the plays of such successful dramatists as Arthur Wing Pinero and Henry Arthur Jones were printed only for the use of the actors and of course were printed in the shorthand of the stage. Then along came Mr. Shaw, announcing himself as a literary dramatist. He scarcely needed to prove his point; for there were his books to prove it for him. The public got an idea that his plays must be literature because they were bound in cloth and sold for two dollars; whereas, obviously, the plays of Pinero and Jones could not be literature, because they were issued in paper covers and sold for fifty cents. To this day, that prejudice exists; and, for many years, there was a doubt in many minds about the literary value of the plays of J. M. Barrie, until the author at last permitted them to appear in print.

The early plays of Mr. Shaw, however literary they might seem upon the printed page, did contain a number of excellent acting parts; and this fact was first discovered by a great American actor. Richard Mansfield discovered "Arms and the Man" shortly after it was published, and produced the play in this country in 1894. This was the first important production of any play of Mr. Shaw's anywhere in the world; and the author had, at that time, already reached the age of thirty-eight. "Arms and the Man" was only mildly successful; but three years later, in 1897, Mr. Mansfield produced "The Devil's Disciple," with more fortunate results. Mr. Mansfield also put into rehearsal the play called "Candida," but abandoned it because he found that the part of Marchbanks was not suited to him. Perhaps it would have been more fair to the author if I had said that the actor was not suited to the part; but, at any rate, the two were incompatible. Thus far, Mr. Shaw had accomplished nothing whatsoever in the theatre of London; and nothing further happened to him in the American theatre until the play called "Candida" was produced in 1903.

This production, from the practical point of view, marked the turning point in Mr. Shaw's career. An exceedingly able, but at that time comparatively unknown, actor happened to "see himself"—as theatre people say—in the rôle of the young poet, Marchbanks. His name was Arnold Daly. He wanted to play that part; but, of course, no manager would let him. In the first place, no manager, in those days of the star system, believed that an unknown actor could carry a play to success; and in the second place, since the play had been published as literature, the managers were sure that there must be something the matter with it. So Mr. Daly, rebuffed at every turn, decided that he would have to do the play himself, although his capital amounted to little more than a hundred dollars. Fortunately, "Candida," though a hard play to act, was a very easy play to put on. It required only a single simple set, which could be borrowed from a scenic storehouse; and, in those days, it was possible to hire a small theatre for a couple of matinée performances at a very small expense. Also, Mr. Daly was able to persuade some of his friends to play the other parts without salary; and they got together and rehearsed,—Dorothy Donnelly as Candida, Dodson Mitchell as Morell, Ernest Lawford as Lexy, Louise Closser Hale as Prossie, and Herbert Standing as Candida's father. Nevertheless, this dauntless little band of players discovered that they would need two or three hundred dollars more to place "Candida" before the public; and Mr. Daly had to hunt up a friend who had two hundred dollars and take him into partnership. This friend, also, was an inconspicuous actor that nobody had ever heard of. His name was Winchell Smith.

They produced "Candida" at a special matinée in 1902; and it made a sensation. At first it was played for two or three matinées a week, at one theatre after another; then it got into an evening bill and ran successfully for weeks and months. It established the fame of Mr. Shaw as a practical playwright and destroyed the managerial superstition that his plays were too literary to be popular. Also, this production achieved a great deal of notoriety for Mr. Arnold Daly, and ruined him for life. He is an admirable actor; but he has never been the same since. Mr. Winchell Smith was affected somewhat otherwise. He took to writing plays; and he is now a millionaire. When Mr. Daly, as a result of the initial run of "Candida," found himself in possession of the price of a steamer ticket, he sailed to England to see Mr. Shaw. Mr. Shaw and Mr. Daly got along very well together, because each of them admitted that both of them were geniuses; and the actor came back to New York and produced several Shaw plays in quick succession,—"The Man of Destiny," "How He Lied to Her Husband," "You Never Can Tell," and "Mrs. Warren's Profession." "Mrs. Warren" was pulled by the police; and that was an excellent ad for both the actor and the author.

In due time, all this was heard about in London; and it occurred to a very bright young man over there that he might do, three or four years afterward, what Mr. Daly had already done. So he hunted up a partner, and hired a theatre, and produced several plays of Mr. Shaw's. He acted the chief parts himself and directed the performances. The name of this young man was Mr. Granville Barker. It was he who made Mr. Shaw successful on the boards of London; and it was this accomplishment that started him on his own remarkable career.

About the same time, Mr. Shaw was discovered in Germany. They liked him very much in Germany, and they still like him very much, because, like the Prussian military leaders, he is entirely intelligent and thoroughly destructive. Also, he tells them frankly that he is better than Shakespeare; and in Germany the people like to know whom to salute.

Mr. Shaw's early plays were all pretty good, and some of them were very good. Make no mistake about that,—even if you *have* just seen "Saint Joan"! I think that "Candida"—which I still regard as the masterpiece of Mr. Shaw—is a great play; and you will remember that "great" is an adjective which I very rarely use. "The Devil's Disciple" is a very good play; so is "Cæsar and Cleopatra"; so is "Man and Superman." So, also, are several of the one-act plays,—notably, "The Showing-Up of Blanco Posnet." When you see Mr. Shaw's bad plays, like "Heartbreak House" or "Back to Methuselah," don't allow yourself to be prejudiced against him. Remember that he used to write good plays,—before he became too proud to write.

The trouble with him, in his later years, arises from the fact that he attained his popular success in a peculiar way. He became successful by gathering around himself a special audience; and that was bad for him. I remember a conversation on the subject of Mr. Shaw that I happened to have in the year 1910 with Sir Arthur Pinero. Mr. Shaw had just written a couple of appallingly bad plays, which had failed in London,

—although, later, they made a little money in the United States. These plays were called "Getting Married" and "Misalliance." "Getting Married" is bad enough; but "Misalliance" is one of the worst plays that have been written within the limits of my memory,—and my memory is more extensive than that of Mr. Heywood Broun. I asked Sir Arthur Pinero what was the matter with Mr. Shaw; and Sir Arthur answered, "He is being hampered by a special audience that always expects him to do the unexpected. He ought to produce a play anonymously. Then he could get rid of his special audience and appeal to the entire public." That is precisely what Mr. Shaw did the following season. He wrote a good play and produced it anonymously; and it achieved a notable success. It was called, you will remember, "Fanny's First Play"; and it was written in the old-fashioned manner of his earlier compositions. "Androcles and the Lion," two years later, was another fine piece of work; but, after that, Mr. Shaw turned lazy again; and, in his later years, he has not bothered to build plays but has merely written reams and reams of endless dialogue.

The work of Mr. Bernard Shaw may, and must, be criticized from two totally different points of view. He must be studied as a playwright, and he must be studied as a propagandist; for he does not write plays for the sake of writing plays but for the sake of propaganda. In his youth, he joined the Fabian Society,—an organization to further the amelioration of social conditions by enlightened legislation. He became a cart-tail orator in Hyde Park; and he has never lost the habit of using the stage as a cart-tail. Thus, people who do not admire his prowess as a dramatist may enjoy his subject-matter, and other people who are bored by his subject-matter may admire his prowess as a dramatist.

For convenience, I shall first set aside his subject-matter and consider him solely as a playwright; and I shall examine his work as a playwright from the point of view of construction, from the point of view of characterization, and from the point of view of writing.

As a builder of plays, Mr. Shaw has demonstrated a genuine ability, whenever he has not been too lazy or too proud to demonstrate it. He began by pouring new wine into old bottles. What he had to say was new, but his technical formula was old. In his early pieces, he followed the traditional and conventional pattern of the well-made play. From the technical point of view, it might be said that his first half dozen plays were patterned in the manner of T. W. Robertson. The ideas were novel, the characters were unusual, but the technical method was Robertsonian. "Candida" might be described as a Robertson play written by another mind,—a keener and more brilliant mind than Robertson's. For instance, the bibulous father of the heroine is introduced solely for the sake of comic relief. I have never believed that he was really Candida's father; and I don't think the author would have pretended that such a daughter could have sprung from such a parent if he had been able to think of any other way to get the comic old man into the pattern of the play. Though Mr. Shaw never rivalled Sir Arthur Pinero as a master of structural technique, he built plays soundly and built them well for many years, and showed that he had learned his job. Then, when he became a fashionable dramatist, he decided that it would look cleverer to build plays as badly as possible, and adopted the new manner of "Getting Married" and "Misalliance." He assumed, somewhat impudently, that the public and the reviewers that had praised and flattered him might not distinguish between his good plays and his bad, or, if they did distinguish, might praise the bad plays for the sake of their novelty and unconventionality; and this, in fact, was what actually happened. At his best, Mr. Shaw, as a craftsman in construction, is not nearly so able as Sir Arthur Pinero, and he is not so able as Mr. Henry Arthur Jones; but he knows enough about the subtle craft of making plays to render quite unpardonable such a shoddy piece of workmanship as "Misalliance."

Now let us turn to the second point of his technique as a playwright,—the matter of characterization. I have said already that his mind is critical rather than creative; but I trust you will regard that statement as definitive rather than condemnatory. The able critic and the able creator are really trying to accomplish the same thing. Both of them are trying to get at the truth of life. The only difference between the creator and the critic is a difference in the direction of their thought. The critic—like Aristotle—tries to get at the truth of life by analysis,—that is, by taking the elements of life apart; and the creator—like Euripides—tries to get at the truth of life by synthesis,— that is, by putting the elements of life together. While creative dramatists—like Barrie, like Pinero, like, in his way, Mr. Galsworthy—are putting the elements of life together so that life results in living people who step forth upon the stage, Mr. Shaw pulls his puppets apart and vivisects his characters before our very eyes. Once or twice he has created a living character and has managed to leave that character alone; but very rarely. Almost never can we imagine the puppets in a Shaw play as existing beyond the limits of the play in which they figure. I have met Pinero's Iris many times in life, but I have never met any of the people of Mr. Shaw. In "Getting Married," he brings on a green-grocer, and this character is asked to describe his wife. He answers, very wittily, "She's a wonderful wife and mother. That's why all my children ran away from home." Now, as soon as he says that, we know that he is not a green-grocer. Green-grocers do not talk like that. It is the author talking, through a ventriloquial puppet. Again, in "Pygmalion," the father of the heroine is made to describe himself as "one of the undeserving poor"; but we know that people of that class do not talk that way about themselves. It is the author, writing a critical essay on the character and putting this essay into the puppet's mouth. In "Saint Joan," time and time again, Mr. Shaw makes his heroine say things about herself that Joan of Arc could never possibly have said. Mr. Shaw can tell us all about a character; but he cannot create a character that needs no critical analysis. In particular, he cannot create women,—for other reasons that I shall come to later on.

I don't think I need say very much about the third point in Mr. Shaw's equipment as a playwright,—the matter of his writing. Everybody agrees that he is a wonderful writer of dialogue. His dialogue is very nearly as humorous as that of Mr. Henry Arthur Jones; it is very nearly as witty as that of Oscar Wilde; and it is just as clever as that of Sir Arthur Pinero. Of course, it is rhetorical and artificial; but I have never believed that it is the province of the playwright to ape the casual and formless flow of actual conversation. It is a pleasure to listen to the rhetoric of Mr. Shaw, except when he becomes too fluent and goes on for hours; and, as a talker, he enjoys the great advantage of being an Irishman.

Now, let me shift our point of view and regard Mr. Shaw, briefly, as a propagandist; for, after all, he is more interested in what he has to say than he has ever been in his medium for saying it. He is evidently quite sincere in regarding himself as a great man; but, to my mind, he seems a useful propagandist rather than an important one. If I were in great trouble and needed the advice of one of the wisest men in the world, I don't think that I should go to Mr. Shaw.

The first habit of his mind that we may note is his habit of always allying himself with what I may call the other side of any subject. If this audience should be divided into two factions, if two hundred and fifty of you should sit on one side of the room and only fifty of you should sit on the other side, and if Mr. Shaw should enter the room, he would sit instinctively on the side of the minority. That may be because he is an Irishman. He always tries to be a champion of unpopular causes, preferably of lost causes; but he forgets that unpopular causes are sometimes—I do not say always—lost because they are wrong. If he ever found the majority on his side, he would feel so uncomfortable that he would have to change his mind. You might have thought that his instinct for the under dog would have led him, in 1914, to champion Belgium against Prussia; but he couldn't do that when all England was preparing to die upon the Belgian side. He fights for the minority not because it is right but because it is the minority.

Another habit of his mind which is only slightly different from that is his habit of telling what I may call the other half of a truth. Of course, most of the ideas and most of the principles which, in this world, are commonly accepted as true are in reality only half true; and it is greatly to the credit of Mr. Shaw that he desires always to point out the other half of the truth. But, in his application of this purpose, he usually goes too far; he insists that his other half of the truth is the whole truth and thereby ends up with a statement that is just as false as the statement that he is combatting. Until Mr. Shaw wrote "Man and Superman," it had been traditionally assumed for several centuries that, in what used to be called the love chase of the sexes, it was the men who pursued the women. Mr. Shaw took a look at this assumption and said, in "Man and Superman,"—"Not at all! It is the women who pursue the men." Now, of course, the whole truth is that they pursue each other, running marathons around an oval track, so that it is impossible to tell which is out in front and which is hurrying after. Whenever Mr. Shaw states the other half of any truth, the sane thing to do is to add his statement to the conventional statement that he is combatting, and then divide by two.

Another habit of his mind is the habit of looking at customary things from an uncustomary point of view. This is, I think, his most salutary habit. All of us are likely to cease to see anything with which our eyes have become too familiar. For more than twenty years—ever since I looked upon it first—I have wanted to own, beyond all other objects in the world, Giovanni Bellini's picture of the Madonna in the Frari Church in Venice; but, if somebody should give it to me, I suppose that, after a month or two, I should walk in and out of the room and never look at it at all. Familiarity may not breed contempt; but at least it strikes us blind. The customary things of

life, that are about us every day, are so familiar that
we do not see them. The only way to make us see
them is to force us to adopt an uncustomary point of
view in looking at them. It occurred to Mr. Shaw
that I would look once more at my Madonna of the
Frari if, on entering the room some day, I should find
the picture hanging upside down; and it occurred to
him that, if he turned all life upside down, he would
force people to see in life things that they had never
seen before. Children know all about this process.
Haven't you seen them bending down and looking at
the world between their legs? In most of Mr. Shaw's
plays, he gives us a topsy-turvy view of life. He
turns the world upside down. Now, this is an illumi-
nating process; but I think that we are likely to grow
a little dizzy when it is practiced without variation.

Another habit of Mr. Shaw's is the zest with which
he snaps up new ideas. He is not an original thinker;
but he quickly arrays his mind with all the latest
thoughts that are launched into the world. That is a
dangerous thing for a dramatist to do; because a new
idea is likely to wear a date upon its forehead, like
the latest issue of a newspaper. Whatever is up to
date to-day is likely to be out of date to-morrow. When
Mr. Shaw, in a new play, deals with the latest ideas
of the moment, he is often dealing with ideas that
the world will have forgotten a dozen years from now.
Do you remember "The Philanderer," which was written in 1893? In that play, Mr. Shaw satirized "the
new woman." Do any of you now remember "the

new woman" of the eighteen-nineties,—that old-fashioned creature that the world forgot long before the war? The trouble with a number of Mr. Shaw's plays, especially with those that deal with the most advanced ideas, is that they will be obsolete in fifty years. The only way to write plays that will live a century from now is not to put into them any reference to current modes of thought. The story of Cinderella will be just as much alive three hundred years from now as it is to-day. It contains no political ideas, or social ideas, or religious ideas that are timely now and will be old-fashioned then. But I can't imagine any interest three hundred years from now in "John Bull's Other Island" or in "Major Barbara."

Finally, we have to note the very important fact that Mr. Shaw, in the habit of his mind, is exclusively intellectual. He seems to me to have an abnormal mind, and in a sense a monstrous mind; and the trouble with his mind is that it is excessively—and at times almost insanely—intelligent. Let us not forget the fundamental psychologic fact that the normal mind functions in three ways,—not one. It thinks with the intellect, it thrills with the sensations, and it feels with the emotions. Mr. Shaw's mind can only think. He himself has stated that he is physiologically deficient in the apparatus of sensation. Consequently he is also deficient in the capacity for emotion. What other people feel, he has to apprehend with his intelligence. It must be rather awful to have a mind that can't do anything but think; because there is nothing individual or personal in the processes of logic. Anybody who thinks his way through the ancient syllogism, that John is mortal because all men are mortal and John is a man, arrives at the logical conclusion by the same process and has exercised no more individuality than an adding machine. The only creations of the mind that may be regarded as individual and personal achievements are the products of sensation and emotion. I am not satisfied with Descartes' syllogism, "I think: therefore I am." I believe that Descartes ought to have said, "I feel: therefore I am." The wisdom of old wives is an emotional wisdom; and so is the wisdom of all the sages of the world.

All that the intellect can do, Mr. Shaw's mind can do; but what the emotions can do is outside his element. He does not believe in anything that is not intelligent. He does not believe in religion. He does not believe in poetry. He does not believe in love. He has never experienced love in his lifetime of sixty-eight years; but he knows that the mind, under the influence of love, does not work in an intellectual manner, and he therefore dismisses love as ridiculous. From the intellectual point of view, it unquestionably is. The love scenes in the plays of Mr. Shaw are written with intelligence to show how silly the lovers are. It was not in that mood that Shakespeare wrote the balcony scene of "Romeo and Juliet." This is, of course, the main reason why Mr. Shaw cannot draw the character of women. Women, though by no means deficient in intelligence, are often more emotional than intellectual; and that is a mood of mind that Mr. Shaw is incapable of understanding. He makes his women monsters of exaggerated intelligence.

In closing, I should like to say that it has not been my purpose to deny, nor to belittle, the extraordinary abilities of Mr. Bernard Shaw. I have sought, merely, to define them. I do not think that he is a great dramatist, because I do not think that he is a creator; but I have repeatedly admitted my admiration for his critical intelligence.

Next week—for the sake of contrast—we shall drift to the other extreme and consider the work of a dramatist who writes plays with his emotions and with no display of intelligence whatsoever. His intellect is not nearly so brilliant as that of Mr. Bernard Shaw; but he knows what every woman knows. Meanwhile, you might read over a play or two by Sir James Barrie.

# SIR JAMES MATTHEW BARRIE

## MARCH 3, 1924

A WEEK ago, I analyzed the mind of Mr. Bernard Shaw and criticized his contributions to the drama. In doing so, I admitted that he is the most intelligent playwright now writing in our language and that he is endowed with one of the most brilliant intellects that are finding expression at the present time in literature. In saying this, I not only praised him but dispraised him. I emphasized what is at once his most obvious merit and also his most obvious defect. I went on to say that his mind is exclusively intellectual, that it is comparatively incapable of coping with matters of sensation or emotion, that he has to translate sensibilities and emotions into intellectual terms before his mind can deal with them, and that there is something unnatural in such a mind, something abnormal, something almost monstrous. This morning, for the sake of contrast and by way of mutual illustration, I am going to talk about the mind of Sir James Barrie, who appears to write his plays without intelligence; for, if he has an intellect and uses it, he manages to conceal the fact, like a clever woman when she manages to get around you. He is an author who is interested mainly in emotions and sensibilities and who seems to address himself directly to the sensibilities and the emotions of the audience. Doubtless he knows, as well as you do, that bodies in space attract each other with a force that varies inversely as the square of the distance between them, and that $(a+b) \times (a-b) = a^2 - b^2$; but you would never catch him letting on to that. But when you are planning to elope with your lady love, he will advise you that you had better wait until Saturday, because that's the day the laundry comes home.

The main reason why Mr. Shaw is overpraised at the present time—particularly by the "young intellectuals," as I believe they call themselves—and the main reason why so little is said about the work of J. M. Barrie in the literary columns that are most fashionable at the moment, is that, for some reason or other, we have blundered into a period in which the intellect is over-honored. We appear to be living in a period when people in general think that the intellect is a very wonderful faculty, while they pay comparatively little attention to the mental accomplishments of the sensibilities and the emotions. I think that this is very unfortunate. The intellect is the most mechanical of the mental faculties and therefore, in my opinion, the least remarkable, the least wonderful, the least miraculous. Has it never occurred to you that nobody in all history has ever at any time been willing to die for an intellectual idea? People are willing to die—or to live—only for emotional ideas; and the more unreasonable, the more unintelligent these ideas are, the more devotedly will people live or die for them. Can you imagine an army going forth with banners to fight for the proposition that the square of the hypothenuse of a right-angled triangle is equal to the sum of the squares on the other two sides? What ideas *do* men fight for?——Ideas of the sort that are sneered at by the intellectuals, ideas about home and mother, about honor, about some flag or other, about God. The only propositions men will die for are propositions that cannot be demonstrated to the intellect, propositions that cannot be proved. Men will die for Joan of Arc, men will die for Rheims Cathedral, men will die for Edith Cavell; but no man ever died for Euclid or Sir Isaac Newton. Consequently, when people devote their attention mainly to intellectual arguments, proving this and demonstrating that and ending up with a Q.E.D., it seems to me that their mental occupation is a comparatively minor one. Who would not rather have said, "Lafayette, we are here," than have been the first man in the world to prove that the whole is equal to the sum of its parts?

I am afraid that the main fault with our educational system at the present time is that it is directed too exclusively toward the development of the intellect. Of course, I have been wondering for many years what is the matter with our educational system. I remember how George Cary Eggleston used to say in his old age that he had spent four years in college and had spent the next fifty years seeking a cure for education. I am afraid that our schools and colleges devote too much attention to the development of the intellect. I dare say that the reason why they do that is that it is comparatively easy to develop the intellect. Anybody can teach plane geometry, anybody can learn it. Anybody can demonstrate that water is composed of two parts of hydrogen and one of oxygen, and anybody can acquire that item of information without imaginative effort. Things that are easy to teach and things that are easy to learn occupy most of the time in our curriculum. It seems to me that we do not devote nearly enough attention to educating and developing the sensibilities and the emotions of the growing mind. Our pupils are made to study diagrams upon a blackboard; but we do not teach them how to look through magic casements opening on the foam of perilous seas in faery lands forlorn.

I suppose that, at this very hour, in this university, hundreds of students in hundreds of rooms are sitting like passive buckets to be pumped into—as Carlyle described the process—while scores of professors are pouring information into them. That seems to me, for the most part, a waste of time. I have never seen any reason why anybody should store his mind with information. It must occupy storage room and may possibly crowd out of the mind something else of greater value. What is the use of remembering the date when Columbus discovered America? If you ever need to know the date—to decide a bet, for instance,—you can step to the nearest encyclopedia, look it up, write it down, and then forget it again. It's right there in the book,—available at any time. If it is in the encyclopedia, why carry it in your head? The only thing worth carrying in our head about Columbus would be something that you could not find in the encyclopedia,—whether or not he cursed when he faced the mutineers, or how he looked when land was sighted, or what he said when he bent his knees in prayer and kissed the new earth that he had discovered. We spend four years in college acquiring a lot of facts, about physics and chemistry and economics and history and philosophy and heaven knows what else; yet I have often wondered why. All these facts are in the books, and all the books are in the library; and we could easily get at them at any time. Why not spend three or four years working our way across the seas to India, so that we might see the Taj Mahal by moonlight?

Of course, I must admit that the intellect must be given a proper amount of exercise, because it is the executive faculty of the mind. The sensibilities bring to the mind tidings of the universe in which we live. The mind reacts to these tidings; and these reactions are emotions. Emotions demand action; and then, of course, the question arises,—What are we to do? This question should be answered by the intellect. It is the intellect which analyzes, judges, orders, and commands the other faculties of the mind. Of course, the intellect must be developed by experience; and it cannot do anybody any harm to study logic or to spend a year or two with Aristotle. But a mind in which only the intellect is developed is something like a Central American army,—an army in which everybody is a general,—a commander with no troops to command.

I am saying all this because, on this particular morning, it is my privilege to recommend to you the work of J. M. Barrie, who is a man who knows how to educate the emotions. When they made him Rector of St. Andrews University, he got up and made a speech that seems to me more educative than any lecture I have ever listened to at Columbia, where we seem to be so proud of our intelligence. Unless my etymology is at fault, the word "educate" means "to lead out of." Please note that it does *not* mean "to pour into." You cannot educate a passive bucket. The delivery of information to a receptive mind—whether in retail or in wholesale lots—is not education. You cannot educate anybody unless, and until, you manage to lead something out of him. Education results from his response to a mental stimulant. An intellectual appeal is rarely educative; but an emotional appeal almost always is. An emotional appeal arouses the entire mind of the person to whom it is addressed. His imagination is stimulated; and, when that stimulus occurs, his mind is forced to express itself by creating something. This something that his mind creates,—this something that is led out of his mind by his response to an emotional appeal,—may be something that he has known subconsciously all the time, without knowing that he knew it. People who

can haul things up out of other people's minds, as
magicians can haul rabbits out of hats, are educators.
I do not think that Mr. Bernard Shaw is much of
an educator; but I am certain that Sir James Barrie is.

An indication of the limitation of the mind of Mr.
Shaw is the fact that he is forever arguing.  He is
never happy unless he is engaged in an intellectual
contention.  But you will observe that the really great
minds never argue at all.  They do not have to.  Regarding a particular proposition that is within their
province, they know that the thing is so or they know
that it is not so; they state the truth about it, and you
may take it or leave it; but they will not waste time
and energy in arguing.  When we read over the four
gospels, we do not find Jesus arguing about religion.
People came to Him with all kinds of religious con-
tentions; but He merely said,—"You talk about a
great many commandments,—ten or a dozen.  There
are only two:  Thou shalt love thy God, and thou
shalt love thy neighbor as thyself."  What was there
to argue about?  A knowledge so serene as that is an
absolute knowledge, because it is a knowledge in which
the entire mind participates,—not merely one part of
the mind, not merely the intellectual, the logical, the
reasoning faculty.

Now Mr. Shaw, when he writes a play and employs
the stage of the theatre as a cart-tail, tries to tell people
things that they did not know before.  He seeks to
startle the intelligence of his auditors by giving them
something new to think about; and that is, in this

motor cars, but they always manage to educate their children.

Barrie began to write in his early twenties; and what he wrote was little sketches of the people he had known at home. At that time, there was no market for writing of this sort. Nearly all the magazines were edited in London, and none of the editors took any interest in the people of Kirriemuir. They objected particularly to the fact that Barrie wrote in the Scottish dialect. They said that nobody could understand it. Because of this, it was some time before he got a start. Nevertheless, he persisted in his purpose; and by the end of his twenties he had managed to place the little town of Thrums on the map of the literary world. In 1888 and 1889, he published two or three volumes of sketches and short stories, including "Auld Licht Idylls" and "A Window in Thrums." "My Lady Nicotine" followed in 1890. Apropos of this book, a point is suggested to me which is of considerable importance. This point is that, when he wrote "My Lady Nicotine," Barrie had never smoked in his life. This fact is so characteristic of the habit of his mind that I shall have to develop the point later on. Throughout his whole career, he has written most knowingly about matters which he has never actually experienced. When you find him writing about something with the utmost fondness and the utmost intimacy, you may infer that that thing is something he has never actually known. He writes about children with extreme fondness and extreme intimacy; but he has never had any children. At the time when he wrote "My Lady Nicotine," as I have said, he had never smoked in his life. He has smoked ever since, however. When the book was published, he read it over; and it was so appealing in its celebration of the charms of smoking that he took up tobacco at once.

In 1891 he wrote a very popular novel, "The Little Minister." You may remember that it was the fashion in the eighteen-nineties to dramatize nearly every popular novel that came along; but all the experts at that kind of craftsmanship told Barrie that "The Little Minister" could not be dramatized. There wasn't any play in the book. Consequently, he dramatized it himself a little later on; and, as you know, it was enormously successful. The most important of his novels, "Sentimental Tommy," came in 1896. It is a study of the development of the artistic temperament in childhood; and every woman ought to read it before making up her mind to marry a literary man. "Tommy and Grizel" followed in 1900; and Barrie's last book, "The Little White Bird," was published in 1902. Thereafter, he ceased to write fiction; for, by that time, he had become thoroughly engrossed with the theatre.

It was early in the eighteen-nineties that Barrie began to try his hand at writing plays,—a task for which, apparently, he had had no preparation whatsoever. The very fact that he had established himself as a novelist and had attained recognition as a man of